DOG DAYS

A Scrapbook for My Best Friend

Illustrated by Kate Madsen

GIBBS·SMITH
P
PUBLISHER

Salt Lake City

03 02 01 00 99 5 4 3 2 1

Copyright © 1999 Gibbs Smith, Publisher

All rights reserved. No part of this book may be reproduced by any means whatsoever, either mechanical, electronic or digital, without written permission from the publisher.

Published by
Gibbs Smith, Publisher
P.O. Box 667
Layton, Utah 84041

Orders: (1-800) 748-5439
Web site: www.gibbs-smith.com

ISBN 0-87905-895-1

Book design and production by Denise Kirby
Printed and bound in Korea

This book is dedicated to

_____
(your dog's name)

What doting dog owner has not been touched by his/her pooch's loyalty, charmed by its personality, delighted by its antics?

This scrapbook provides a fun way for you to capture the essence of your canine companion. Be as creative as you like—draw pictures, write of your adventures in prose or poetry, and freeze your dog's best moments in snapshots with witty captions. Make this book your own, and as you add to it over the years, it will record the zaniest times and the most precious times you share together.

paw print

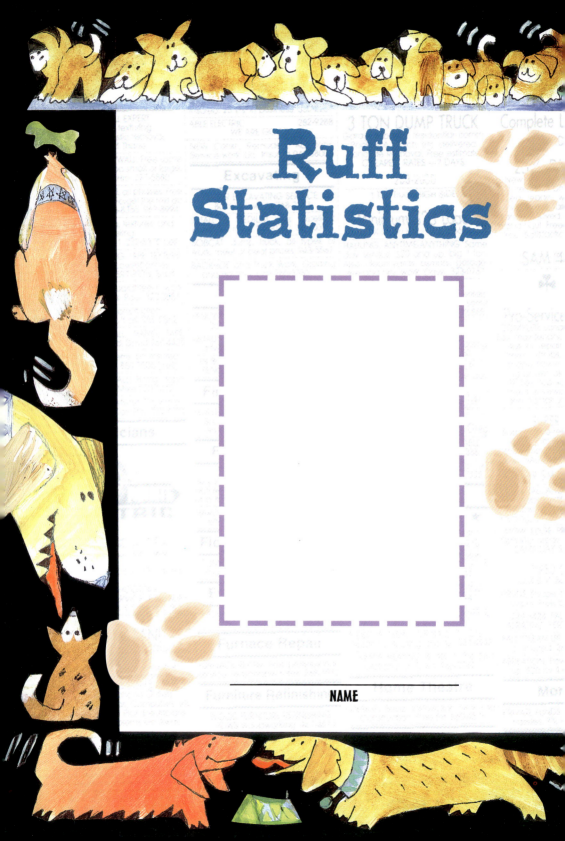

Birth date: _____

Birthplace: _____

Breed: _____

Pedigree: sire: _____

        dam: _____

Age of adoption: _____

Place of adoption: _____

Physical characteristics: _____
_____

Vaccinations and dates:

_____ _____

_____ _____

_____ _____

_____ _____

_____ _____

_____ _____

Relative Canines

(My dog's family of origin and adoption)

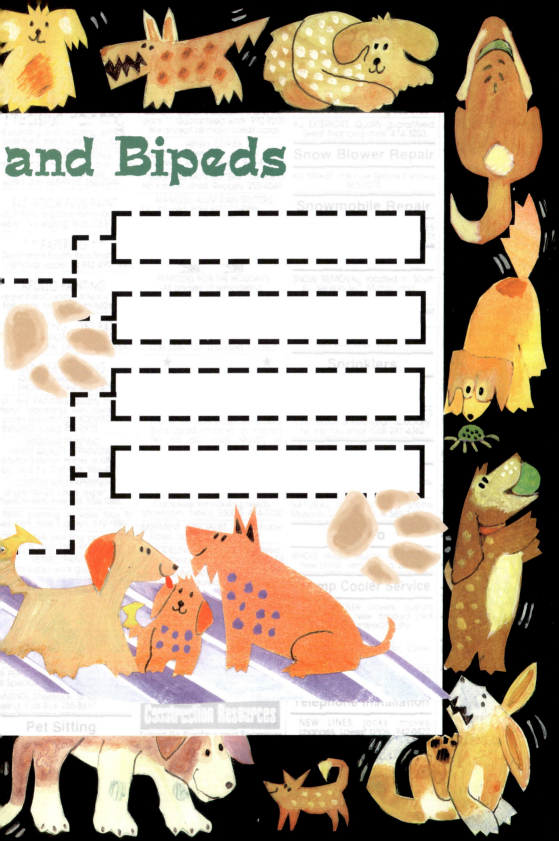

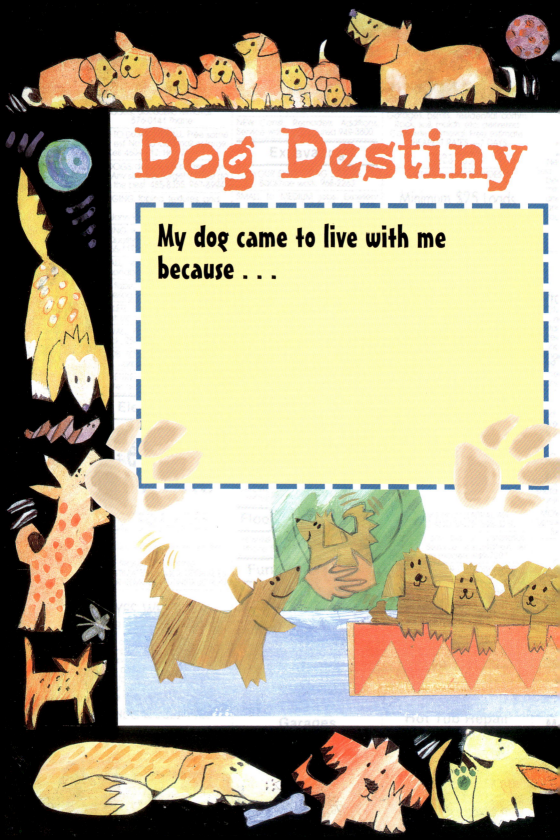

Dog Destiny

My dog came to live with me because . . .

My life was changed by my dog's . . .

Favorite Frozen

Moments

Personality

The Light Side

Personality

The Dark Side

Always an

I like it best when my dog . . .

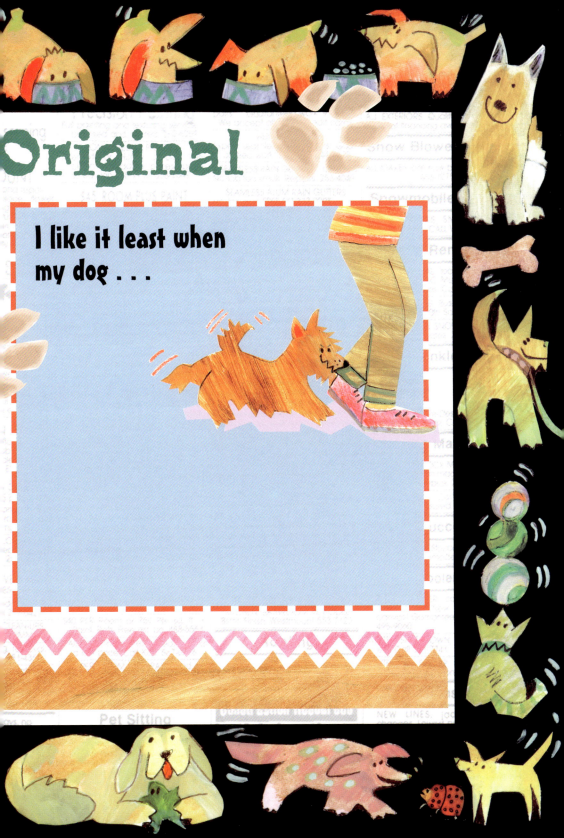

The Comical

I laugh the hardest when . . .

More funny things my dog did . . .

Clever and Cunning

I think my dog displays his/her intelligence when . . .

The Predictable

At the prospect of a car ride, my dog . . .

When we are reunited after a trip or coming home from work . . .

The mail carrier arrives and my dog . . .

When I announce that it is time for a walk . . .

Surprise!

Recognized Words

My dog's ears perk up when I say . . .

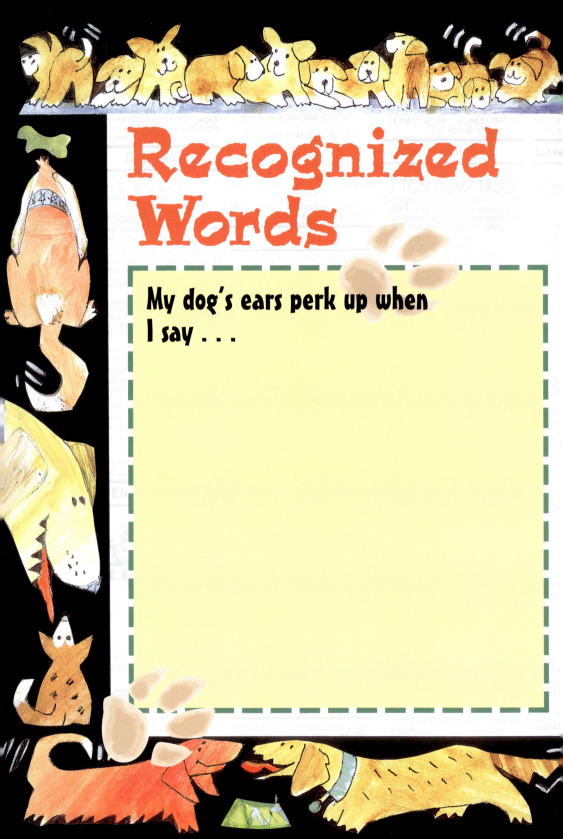

Commands

Ignored . . .

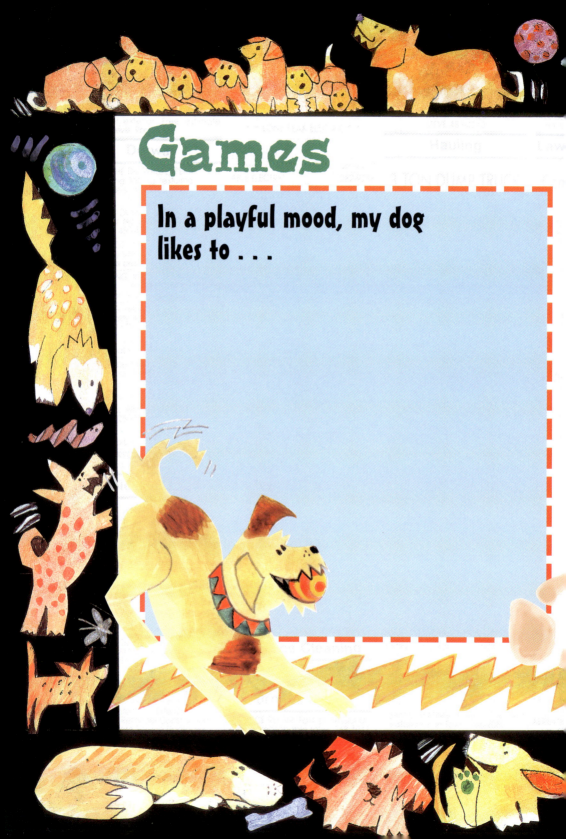

Games

In a playful mood, my dog likes to . . .

Favorite Frozen

Moments

Tricks

I am proudest of my dog when (s)he shows people . . .

I have wonderful memories of the time that my dog . . .

Snoozing Routine

My dog's preferred time and place to slumber . . .

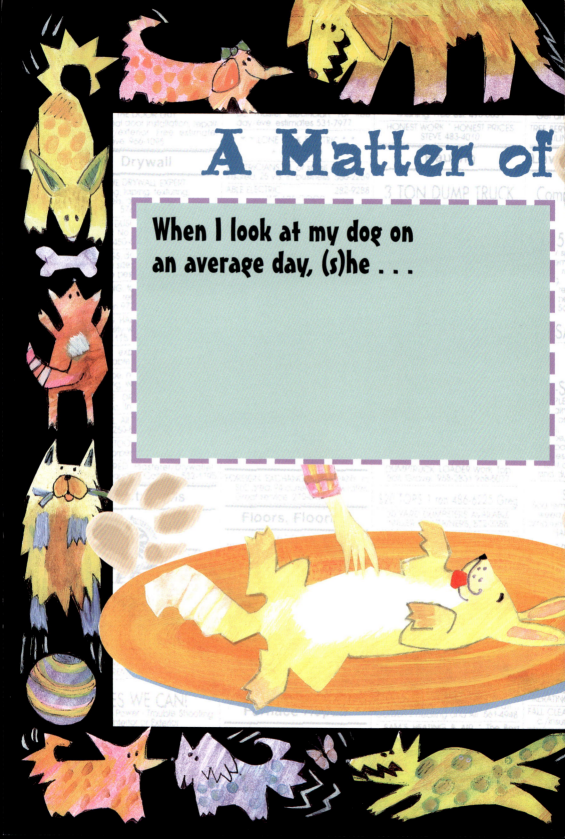

Out in the Air . . .

I'm proud to reveal that my dog . . .

. . . and Under the Rug

I would rather conceal that my dog . . .

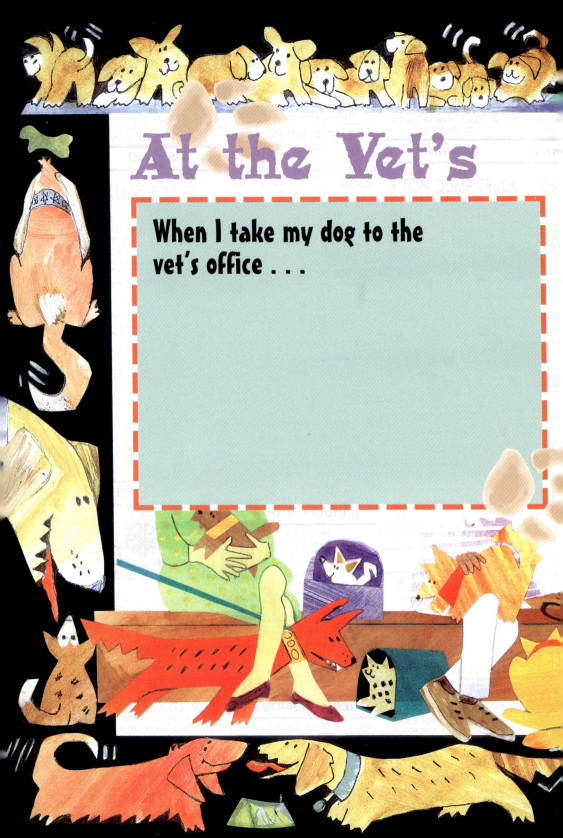

At the Vet's

When I take my dog to the vet's office . . .

The greatest adventure I have had with my canine companion is . . .

Adventures

Briefly Sentimental

My dog is . . .

Sentimental Still

My dog is most unique because . . .

Quirky Attributes

Creature Comfort

If I am feeling low, my dog . . .

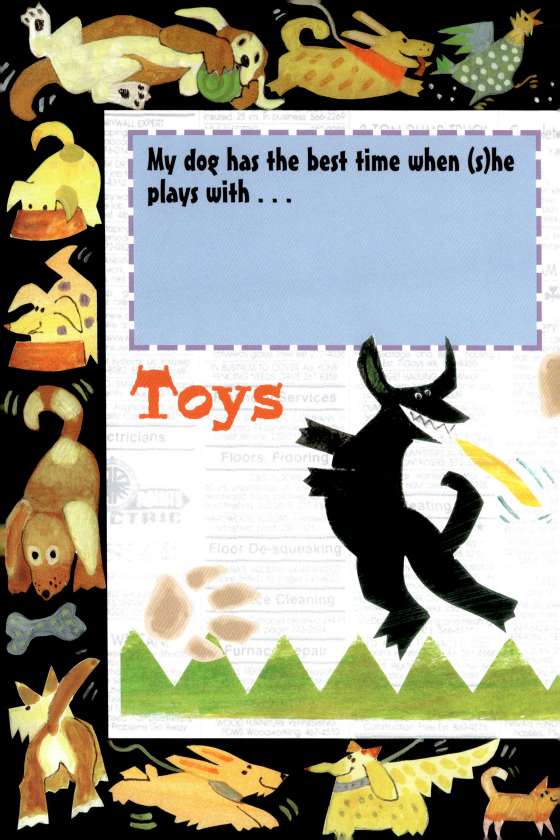

When (s)he is happy, my dog . . .

Communication

When (s)he is angry . . .

When (s)he is sad . . .

When (s)he is scared . . .

Favorite Frozen

PHOTO/ART

Moments

PHOTO/ART

PHOTO/ART

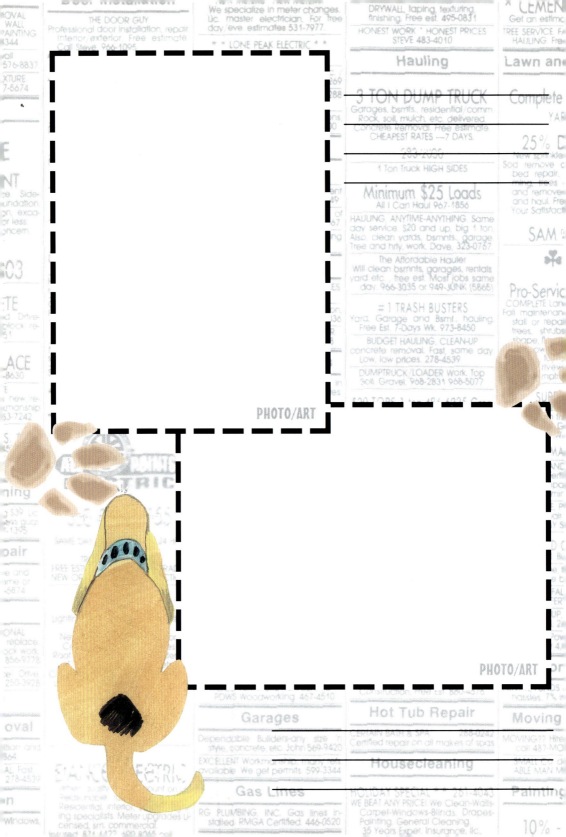